T is for Tar Heel

A North Carolina Alphabet

Written by Carol Crane and Illustrated by Gary Palmer

Sleeping Bear Press
310 North Main Street, Suite 300
Chelsea, MI 48118
www.sleepingbearpress.com

Sleeping Bear Press is an imprint of The Gale Group, Inc.,
a division of Thomson Learning, Inc.

Printed and bound in Canada.

10 9 8 7 6 5 4 3 2

Library of Congress Cataloging-in-Publication Data
Crane, Carol, 1933-
T is for Tar Heel : a North Carolina alphabet / by Carol Crane ;
illustrated by Gary Palmer.
p. cm.
Summary: Presents information about the state of North Carolina
in an alphabetical arrangement.
ISBN 1-58536-082-1
1. North Carolina-Juvenile literature. 2. English language-Alphabet-Juvenile
literature. [1. North Carolina. 2. Alphabet.] I. Palmer, Gary, 1968- ill. II. Title.
F254.3 .C73 2003
975.6—dc21   2003010381

To Sharon Marble, a native Tar Heel, educator, and friend.

CAROL CRANE

*To my wife, Rebecca, for her love and support,
and to my sons, Joel and Evan, for their friendship and inspiration.*

GARY PALMER

The Appalachian Mountains lie within the western North Carolina border. It is one of the oldest mountain ranges in the world. Along the border of North Carolina and Tennessee lie the Great Smoky Mountains. The Blue Ridge Mountains are the eastern mountain range. Emeralds, rubies, garnets, amethyst, and sapphires are found here. The emerald is the official state precious stone, while the official state rock is granite.

In North America, only the forests of the great Northwest receive more rainfall than the Appalachians. The pine tree is the official state tree. There are also black bears, rattlesnakes, hawks, and other wildlife to see. The gray squirrel is the official state mammal.

Rain and downhill mountain terrain have developed 250 spectacular waterfalls. Whitewater Falls is the highest waterfall in the eastern United States. Visitors can slide like playful otters down Sliding Rock Waterfall. This natural 60-foot slide drops you into a cold pool below. What fun!

A is for the Appalachian Mountains,
trees, trails, animals, birds, and flowers.
Nature's green and noble heights,
welcome us in sun and showers.

In 1771 a German historian and scientist reported seeing the mysterious lights on Brown Mountain. The U.S. Geological Survey has investigated these lights. One thing is certain, the lights do exist. The lights show up on the horizon appearing to be the size of a star. Sometimes they have a reddish or blue cast. The lights move near, fade away, and then reappear. On dark nights they pop up so thick and fast it's impossible to count them.

Early frontiersmen believed the lights were the spirits of Cherokee and Catawba warriors. Many North Carolina families head for the mountain at night, waiting to see this awesome sight that no one can explain.

B stands for Brown Mountain Lights,
mysterious star-shaped eerie glow.
Forever moving with a blaze and shimmer,
some say it's ghosts from long ago.

The Cape Hatteras Lighthouse has warned sailors of dangerous shallow sandbars off the Atlantic Ocean coast for more than 100 years. The Diamond Shoals extend 14 miles out into the Atlantic Ocean. The area along the Outer Banks is called the "Graveyard of the Atlantic." Over 2,000 ships have run aground or been lost along this strip of the sea. The lighthouse has spiral striping and has the nickname "The Big Barber Pole." Its beacon of light can be seen 20 miles out at sea. The keeper of the lighthouse had to climb 268 steps to light the lamp.

Whale oil was used to keep the light burning. Today, the light is kept burning by electricity and is not cared for by a lighthouse family. Six lighthouses along the North Carolina coast help sailors get their bearings at sea. Each lighthouse has a different light pattern sending its beacon of light, and each has a different painted design.

C is for the Cape Hatteras Lighthouse, sending a light with great power. Signaling all ships at sea, ever vigilant hour by hour.

Now, **D** is for the Dogwood,
flowers gentle pink and white.
From mountains to city streets,
in spring a showy delight.

The flowering dogwood is the official state flower of North Carolina. Everyone knows spring has finally arrived when the dogwood is in bloom. Many of the blooms have a pink blush while others are pure white. In the center are berries that turn a bright red in the fall. What a sight to see the official state bird, the cardinal, sitting and singing among the abundant flowers in the spring and feasting on the red berries in the fall!

The letter E is for the Eastern Box Turtle,
official reptile of our state.
Moving about with a house on his back,
he doesn't care if he's late!

With a high domed shell and streaks, spots, and lines of yellow and orange, the Eastern Box Turtle is a familiar sight throughout North Carolina. The turtle pulls in his legs and head and closes his shell like a box. This is a cozy house he can escape into when in danger. The mother turtle lays three to six eggs in a warm, dark place and leaves them to hatch on their own. The babies are so small and have none of the bright colors of the adult turtles, so they are hard to see. Box turtles often live 30 to 40 years. Eastern Box Turtles keep our ponds and streams clean. We must protect these reptiles that help our state's environment.

Now, F stands for Flat Rock,
here Rootabaga Stories are told.
The home of America's writer, Carl Sandburg,
sit and listen to the tales unfold.

Carl Sandburg was one of America's great poets and biographers. He won the Pulitzer Prize for his biography of Abraham Lincoln. He also wrote humorous stories for children. Today his home, Connemara, is a National Historic Site. He lived with his family in this house on the hill for 22 years.

When you enter the house, you see bookshelves in every room, with over 10,000 titles on display. Mr. Sandburg was a great reader of other authors' books. Mrs. Sandburg raised prize goats. The National Park Service still maintains the barns and a herd of goats for children to pet. Every summer, in an outdoor theater, students act out his Rootabaga Stories for all to enjoy.

Ef

G is for Grandfather Mountain,
climb atop the mountain so high.
For an added thrill, walk Mile High Bridge,
where you can try to touch the sky.

The first settlers that came to the valleys of the Blue Ridge Mountains named the mountain for the giant bearded man they saw outlined in its ridges. The Cherokee Indians named the mountain "Tanawha" for the golden eagles that rode the wind currents.

Grandfather Mountain is the highest peak in the Blue Ridge. It is also the only private park in the world that has been named by the United Nations as an International Biosphere Reserve. People from all over the world visit this unique mountain. Here they may see rare and endangered species such as the peregrine falcon, Blue Ridge goldenrod, funnelweb tarantulas, ravens, and the Virginia big-eared bat.

Climbing up the mountain, you will reach the Mile High Swinging Bridge. It is the nation's highest suspension footbridge. The wind some days reaches 55 miles per hour. The wind passing through the steel rail tubes makes a humming sound that can be heard a mile away.

H h

An important little insect
gives me honey for my tea.
He works to give us jars of gold—
H is our state's Honeybee.

The honeybee is North Carolina's official state insect. It not only provides us with honey for eating, but this industrious little insect is very important for the pollination of crops in our state. The production of honey gives the state two million dollars' worth of honey to sell every year. There is nothing better than honey on southern biscuits and as a sweetener in tea!

In October each year, the Woolly Worm Festival is held in Banner Elk, North Carolina. The woolly bear caterpillars are gathered here. They are studied and predictions are made for the winter weather. Will it be a very cold winter or a mild one? The woolly worm has black bands at each end of the caterpillar. The band in the middle is brown or orange giving the worm its stripes. According to folklore, the wider the middle brown section is, the milder the coming winter will be. A narrow brown band is said to predict a harsh winter.

The Isabella tiger moth is a medium-sized moth, yellowish orange and cream colored, spotted with black. Its larva is called the woolly bear or woolly worm. They are covered with short, stiff bristles of hair.

Have you ever had a woolly worm climb onto your finger?

I i

Isabella moth caterpillar is our I,
sometimes called the woolly worm.
Will it be a very cold winter or warm?
Old timers check their stripes to confirm.

The 7th president of our country was Andrew Jackson. He was born in a log cabin on the border of North Carolina and South Carolina in 1767. He was known to read the Declaration of Independence to his non-reading neighbors at the age of nine. He was a great leader in the War of 1812. Jackson's soldiers thought he was as tough as an old hickory tree. His nickname from that time on was "Old Hickory."

The 11th president of our country was James Knox Polk. His nickname was "Young Hickory." He was born in Pineville, North Carolina in 1795. President Polk and his wife started the music salute "Hail to the Chief" now associated with the presidency.

The 17th president of the United States was Andrew Johnson. He was born in Raleigh, North Carolina in 1808. During Johnson's time in office, the U.S. purchased Alaska from Russia.

J j

J stands for Presidents Andrew Jackson, James Polk, and Andrew Johnson. Three leaders of our grand nation, honored for their legislation.

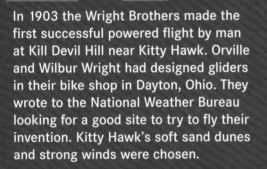

In 1903 the Wright Brothers made the first successful powered flight by man at Kill Devil Hill near Kitty Hawk. Orville and Wilbur Wright had designed gliders in their bike shop in Dayton, Ohio. They wrote to the National Weather Bureau looking for a good site to try to fly their invention. Kitty Hawk's soft sand dunes and strong winds were chosen.

Their first flying masterpiece at Kill Devil Hill was not a glider, but had a gasoline engine. Wilbur was the first to attempt to fly the plane, but he raised the nose too high and down he came. Orville was next. The winds were blowing 27 miles per hour and the plane took off. They made three more flights that day.

North Carolina has a Wright Brothers National Memorial dedicated to honor these two pioneers of flight. The license motto on North Carolina plates reads "First in Flight."

K is for Kill Devil Hill,
where the Wright Brothers first flew their plane.
They chose this place near Kitty Hawk,
for they needed a windy terrain.

L is for the Lost Colony,
a famous mystery case.
The baby, Virginia Dare, and the settlers
disappeared without a trace.

In 1585 Sir Walter Raleigh sent 600 men to Roanoke Island. These settlers built houses and Fort Raleigh. This was England's first North American settlement. This first group of settlers returned to England.

In 1587 a new group of settlers reached Roanoke Island, repaired the fort, and built new houses. Later that year a baby girl was born, named Virginia Dare. She was the first English child born in America. The governor of the colony left and sailed back to England for supplies. He left instructions that if the settlers left the colony they were to carve into a tree where they were going.

When he returned to Roanoke three years later, he found that all the people were gone. The fort and houses had been destroyed. The letters CROATOAN were carved into a tree but there was no sign of the settlers. Believing the settlers had gone off to live with the friendly Croatoan people, he searched but found no colonists.

Ll

M is for Mountain Azaleas,
in spring, we see blazing mountain walls.
And on every crest, flowers blossom,
cascading like colored waterfalls.

Some of the most beautiful natural gardens in the world can be seen in the state of North Carolina. Mountain Azalea blooms are like huge cones of raspberry and pink cotton candy. Rhododendron also decorates the mountainsides.

Some wildflower names found in the mountains are very strange but interesting: trillium, butterfly weed, Dutchman's britches, fairy wand, and Indian pipe are just a few. We must all be careful and protect the wildflowers of our mountains.

m
M

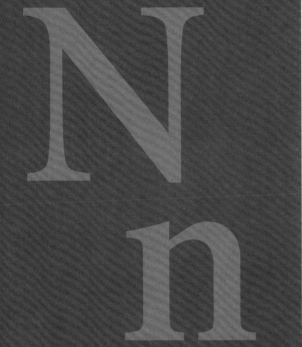

N n

North Carolina pottery is our N, shaped into all designs and sizes. Families since 1700 have turned and molded pieces that are prizes.

Many families of English potters settled in the Seagrove, North Carolina area in the 1700s. They found rich clay deposits. There were also many pine trees, which were needed for red-hot fires in the kilns. Long ago, the potters' shops were the only places to buy pots and storage jars for fruit and milk. They also made butter churns, chamber pots, and dinnerware. Today, the tradition lives on. Seagrove is the home of a pottery museum. Many shops line the streets and alleyways.

O

O is for the Outer Banks,
a fragile strand of shifting, moving sand.
Forever changing from storms and currents,
these barrier islands guard the mainland.

Imagine a thin strip of islands 300 miles long on the Atlantic Ocean. These islands are called the Outer Banks. They protect the land known as the Coastal Plains. Some of the island names are Hatteras, Ocracoke, Topsail, Bodie, and Roanoke. The Cape Hatteras National Seashore and the Pea Island National Wildlife Refuge are wonderful places to see and enjoy wildlife.

The Scotch Bonnet was designated as the state shell and can be found along the North Carolina coastal waters. On Ocracoke Island wild ponies once roamed the dunes and grass flats. These are descendants of Spanish mustangs. Now you can see them being fed regularly and living in a 170 acre pasture.

The shad boat was named the official state historical boat in 1987. These boats, constructed from native trees, are so well made that even 100 years later they are still being used.

Snow Goose

Loggerhead Sea Turtle

Scotch Bonnet

Brown Pelican

Pp

P is for the Plott Hounds,
who are courageous and true.
In the mountains of North Carolina,
hunting bears is what they do.

In 1750 two brothers immigrated to America from Germany and settled in the mountains of North Carolina. When the young boys left Germany they brought with them five hounds. One brother, Johannes George Plott, settled in the Blue Ridge Mountains, married, and raised his family. Since that time, over 200 years, the seven generations of Plotts have raised their dogs. These dogs are fast, bright, and quick to learn. They are used to hunt bear and wild boar. North Carolina officially adopted the Plott Hound as our state dog on August 12, 1989.

Charlotte, North Carolina,
a regal name so pretty.
Honored for King George's wife,
Q is known as our Queen city.

Charlotte, North Carolina is the state's largest city. It was named for Queen Charlotte, the wife of King George III of England.

One important historical event came about one Sunday when a young boy brought home a gold rock he found in the river and used it for a doorstop. A visitor came by the cabin one day and stubbed his toe on the rock. "Gold!" he yelled. The boy's father took the 17-pound stone to a jeweler and received $3.50 for it. The gold rush was on! Today, at the Reed Gold Mine State Historic Site, you may pan for gold.

There are four bronze statues found in Charlotte that tells its historical story: a gold miner illustrates commerce, a female mill worker tells a strong textile heritage, a railroad builder shows Charlotte's transportation center, and a mother lifting her child toward the sky expresses hope for the city's future.

Qq

Now **R** is for Raleigh,
the capital of our state.
It's where our rules and laws are made,
that makes our state so great.

Raleigh became the capital of North Carolina in 1794. It was named after the English explorer Sir Walter Raleigh. The city is located near the Neuse River and is in the hilly Piedmont area in the middle of the state. Raleigh is the second largest city in North Carolina. The Triangle Area is known as Raleigh, Durham, and Chapel Hill. The Triangle refers to the Research Triangle Park between Durham and Raleigh. This area is one of the largest planned research parks in the world.

Raleigh has two main buildings where the government meets. The State Capitol has the governor's office. State senators and representatives meet in the huge State Legislative Building.

Rr

S is for Sweet Potato,
with vitamins A and C.
It is the official vegetable of our state.
Oh! So good for you and me.

North Carolina is the largest producer of sweet potatoes in the nation. It harvests over 4 billion pounds of this vegetable a year. Students from a school in our state petitioned North Carolina's General Assembly to have this golden orange vegetable made the official state symbol. The sweet potato is a member of the morning glory family. The thick, edible roots are the sweet potato. What would Thanksgiving or any other holiday be without a dish of this good vegetable?

Speaking of Thanksgiving, North Carolina also leads the country in the raising of turkeys!

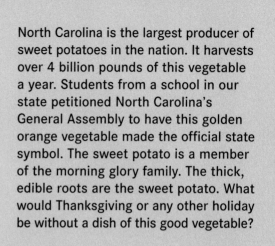

The Civil War was fought from 1861 to 1865. About 125,000 North Carolinians fought for the Confederacy. The Confederate General Robert E. Lee said the state's men stuck to their posts as if held by tar. This may be one of the reasons why North Carolina is called the Tar Heel State.

North Carolina also has had a very important industry, the "naval stores" business. Timber men harvested turpentine, tar, and pitch from pine tree products. These products were used to build and repair ships.

The North Carolina flag is beautiful. The top bar on the flag is red, the bottom bar white, and the flag's field side bar is blue. The top scroll has the date May 20th 1775, which was the start of the Revolutionary War. The bottom date on the scroll is April 12th 1776, when North Carolina became the first colony to vote for independence.

In sports, colleges, and throughout history "Tar Heel" is expressed with pride by fans.

T stands for Tar Heel,
a title that we're all proud of.
Our flag, our ancestors, "good people,"
we honor the history we love.

In 1822 trout fishermen watched trout swimming in and out of Humpback Mountain. When they investigated, they found an opening in the mountain. What they saw was a deep cavern. It is now known as Linville Caverns.

Explorers found Eastern Pipistrelle bats hanging from the ceiling, granddaddy long legged spiders, and cave crickets. Stone icicles formed beautiful shapes throughout the cave. These stone icicles are called stalactites and hang down from the ceiling. Stalagmites grow up from the floor, reaching to the ceiling. There is a constant 52-degree temperature in these caverns.

U u

Deep beneath Humpback Mountain,
bats, spiders, stone icicles too.
Dark tunnels and rooms below,
Underground caverns is our U.

V

Biltmore Mansion with 255 rooms,
magnificent beauty to the hilt.
V   This man loved the surrounding mountains,
so our V stands for George Vanderbilt.

Multimillionaire George Washington Vanderbilt opened the Biltmore Estate on Christmas Eve, 1895. It had taken six years to build. The mansion has 255 rooms, 34 bedrooms, 43 bathrooms, 65 fireplaces, 3 kitchens, and an indoor swimming pool.

The house was very modern for its time. It was wired for electricity when it was constructed, so it had electric lights, central heating, and even refrigerators. There is a three-mile road up to the mansion where forests, parks, and gardens are part of the 8,000 acres. The name Biltmore is a combination of two words. "Bildt" for the region in Holland where the Vanderbilt family came from, and "moor," an old English word meaning upland rolling hills.

Early settlers brought a blend of dancing to the Appalachians. The Irish and Scots brought their jigs. The English came with their dances. The African culture gave us high-kicking dances, and some of the stomp steps came from Native American dances. Put all of these steps together and you have clogging, a blend of dances from many cultures.

The dances vary from hillside to hillside with pride in the different steps. Some of the names of the dances are "Wringing the Chicken's Neck," "Stepping on a Snake," and "Briar Patch." To the music of the fiddle and dulcimer, the dancing comes alive in the cities and mountains of North Carolina.

"Wringing the Chicken's Neck" is our W,
clogging in the old Appalachian tradition.
Skip, shuffle, stomp, and slap your thigh,
start up the fiddlers and dulcimer musician.

X stands for the railroad crossings,
a tiny train chugs around the bends.
Hear the "Tweet, Tweeeet" horn blowing.
The Tweetsie Railroad calling its friends.

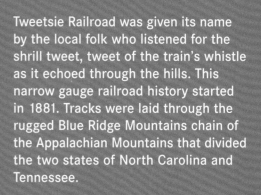

Tweetsie Railroad was given its name by the local folk who listened for the shrill tweet, tweet of the train's whistle as it echoed through the hills. This narrow gauge railroad history started in 1881. Tracks were laid through the rugged Blue Ridge Mountains chain of the Appalachian Mountains that divided the two states of North Carolina and Tennessee.

Iron mines, lumber, and passenger service were all necessary links for transportation through the mountains. The Tweetsie Locomotive #12 was put to rest in 1956. The train was supposed to be shipped out west for use in movies; however, a native of North Carolina bought the little engine for one dollar.

Tweetsie now makes a scenic three-mile loop through the mountains near Blowing Rock. It is one of North Carolina's newest travel attractions where families can enjoy the railroad theme park, and is listed on the National Register of Historic Places.

Now, Y stands for the Yadkin River,
whispering tales from long ago.
Indians, pioneers, and settlers
followed the river's flow.

Y y

The Yadkin River starts its path in the Blue Ridge Mountains, near Blowing Rock. The river crosses North Carolina and becomes known as the Pee Dee River before it ends up in the Atlantic Ocean. The Indians, pioneers, and settlers used Shallow Ford to cross the river. It was the only site shallow enough for early pioneers and settlers with their wagons to cross the river as they traveled down from northern states. This route for the Conestoga wagons was known as the Great Philadelphia Wagon Road in the Yadkin Valley and beyond.

North Carolina's NASCAR races are an event for all ages. NASCAR stands for National Association of Stock Car Auto Racing. North Carolina has several locations where races are held. The drivers become very famous and fans love to cheer their favorites on.

The flags of NASCAR share warnings and updates with drivers who are racing around and around the track. The red flag means the race must be stopped for safety reasons. Crossed flags mean the race is at the halfway point. A black flag means the car must get off the track because there is a problem with the car. The yellow flag means caution and the cars must reduce their speed. The white flag tells the drivers that there is one lap remaining before the end of the race. The checkered flag says that the race has been completed. Whoever crosses the finish line first when this flag is waving is the winner of the race.

Z is for Zoom—Zoom—Zoom,
bright colored cars race round the track.
North Carolina is the home of NASCAR.
Crowds cheering; who will lead the pack?

We've raced through the letters from A to Z,
Let's do it again and see what we can see!

Tar Heel Sticky Questions

1. What city is known as the "City of Medicine?"
2. The *USS North Carolina* is stationed in what city?
3. What is the name of the world's largest military installation?
4. Chinquapin is the birthplace of Caleb D. Bradham, the creator of what famous soft drink?
5. With an elevation of 6,684 feet, what is the name of the highest elevation in eastern America?
6. What is the state's motto and what does it mean?
7. The states official saltwater fish is called...?
8. What states and ocean border North Carolina?
9. Name the manufacturing products that are produced in North Carolina.
10. Street signs and the city flag are adorned with crowns shaped around the letter "M" in what city?
11. A giant granite rock overlooking a gorge and water-falls twice the height of Niagara Falls is in what park?
12. What area is said to be the only place where snow falls upward?
13. In what city did "Babe" Ruth belt his first pro home run in a spring training game in 1914?
14. High Point is known as what?
15. What do we eat at Thanksgiving that North Carolina raises more of than any other state in the United States?
16. Why, in 1774, did the women of Edenton, North Carolina hold the "Edenton Tea Party?"
17. North Carolina would not sign the United States Constitution until what was added?
18. What was the name of two famous pirates that robbed ships along the Carolinas' coast?
19. On November 21, 1789, North Carolina became the twelfth state to join the United States. Also, that same year, it gave up land that became what neighboring state?
20. Who was one of the most famous First Ladies, born in Greensboro?
21. Moses B. Cone was known for his textile mills and an article of clothing we wear almost everyday. What is it?
22. Sir Walter Raleigh provided funds and ships for the first English settlement. Did he ever sail to America?
23. What does "Piedmont" mean?
24. The Blue Ridge Parkway extends through the mountains for how many miles?
25. How did the town of Whynot get its name?

1. Durham. Research Triangle Park, Duke, and North Carolina universities are all located in Durham.
2. The battleship USS North Carolina, "The Showboat," made her way up Cape Fear River and slid majestically into the Port of Wilmington.
3. Fort Bragg was first established in 1918. Today it is the world's largest airborne facility.
4. Creator of Pepsi-Cola.
5. Mount Mitchell is located in Yancey County and has five of the highest peaks east of the Mississippi.
6. "Esse Quam Videri" is the state motto, which means "to be rather than to seem."
7. The Red Drum. Some of these fish weigh more than 40 pounds.
8. Virginia to the north; South Carolina and Georgia to the south; and Tennessee to the west. The Atlantic Ocean is to the east.
9. North Carolina is first in the nation in furniture, textiles, and tobacco products. Other products include computers, machinery, medicine, and chemicals.
10. Charlotte, the Queen City.
11. Chimney Rock Park.
12. The Blowing Rock. Here, lightweight objects thrown over the cliff will return to the thrower when uprising air currents are present.

13. Fayetteville, North Carolina.
14. "Furniture Capital of the World," and also the leading maker of socks and other hosiery.
15. Turkeys and sweet potatoes.
16. The women protested taxes and refused to use British products.
17. The Bill of Rights, which protects freedom of speech and other basic rights.
18. Blackbeard and Stede Bonnet.
19. The state of Tennessee.
20. Dolly Madison was born in Greensboro in 1768.
21. Moses B. Cone was known as the "Denim King." He put the blue in blue jeans.
22. Sir Walter Raleigh himself never crossed the Atlantic. Fort Raleigh and the capital are named after him.
23. "Piedmont" means "Foot of the Mountain."
24. 469 miles of tunnels, bridges and narrow roads were built through the Blue Ridge Mountains. The road took 52 years to complete.
25. The town went nameless for years. The community finally had a debate on what its name should be. "Why not this name?" "Why not that one?" were asked, and it was decided to name the town "Whynot."

Carol Crane

T is for Tar Heel is Carol's 9th book with Sleeping Bear Press. She has authored numerous alphabet books in their Discover America State by State series, from Alaska (*L is for Last Frontier*) to Florida (*S is for Sunshine*) as well as companion counting books including *Sunny Numbers: A Florida Counting Book* and *Round Up: A Texas Numbers Book*. She is widely known for her expertise in children's literature.

From the mountains to the outer banks, Carol has explored all roads leading in and around this great state. A historian and fan of all sports, she lives in Holly Springs, North Carolina with her husband, Conrad, where she can read historical markers and go to football games.

Gary Palmer

Gary Palmer's murals can be seen at the North Carolina Museum of Natural Science. He has also created prints for the North Carolina Nature Conservatory. He has worked in commercial illustration for numerous ad agencies, corporations, and magazine and book publishers.

Gary's home studio in Charlotte overlooks perennial and water gardens in a woodland setting. He is an avid outdoorsman, and has taken regular camping and fishing trips with his family throughout North Carolina. He loves to explore the back roads and trails of the Tar Heel state with his wife, Rebecca and sons Joel and Evan.